Notes on

Music

by Louis R. Torres and Carol A. Torres

Notes on Music

ISBN: 0-9703553-2-7

Published by:

TorresLC Ministries

P.O. Box 688
Gaston, OR 97119

Also distributed by:

Laymen Ministries

414 Zapada Rd.
St. Maries, ID 83861

(208)245-5388
1-800-245-1844

www.lmn.org

Cover design: Terri Prouty
Typeset: Times, 12/14

Contents

Foreword

"Music is one of the few things that universally sways the emotions and behavior of human beings. It can soothe and quiet frayed nerves while lifting the thoughts toward God, or it can arouse deadly passions. Being a master psychologist, Satan uses music to gain entrance to the minds of humans, hypnotizing his victims, and imprisoning them in sin. The concepts presented in these pages regarding music and its power over the human mind and soul should be weighed very carefully by everyone who takes salvation seriously." George E. Rice, Ph. D.

• • •

"I can heartily endorse *Notes On Music* by Louis and Carol Torres. The point of view expressed is one that is not often heard. Louis Torres was a professional rock musician before his conversion to Christ, and he writes from a perspective that is both informed and helpful. His wife, Carol, is a former concert violinist; both are acquainted with the eschatology of music and the role that it has to play, particularly in the days just before Jesus returns. This book may be viewed by some within the church as "a voice crying in the wilderness," but if its message is heeded, it will — like that original New Testament voice — help to "make ready a people prepared for their God." Roger W. Coon, Ph.D.

• • •

"I have been acquainted with Louis and Carol's work for a few years and I am happy to recommend the book, *Notes On Music*. Its content is serious and very much needed." C. Mervyn Maxwell, Professor of Church History, Andrews University.

Meet the Authors

Louis R. Torres — My Story

It was a very humble home life in Puerto Rico that I shared with my parents, four older brothers and one younger sister — so humble that even poverty looked good. Whatever family life we had was soon to be shattered by the separation of my mother and father and the death of my sister, the princess of my life.

After a short time and the addition of a stepfather and a younger brother, my family decided to move to New York City in search of a better life. With enough saved up to move half the family, my stepfather planted my mother, two brothers, and myself in New York and then returned to Puerto Rico to work, save, and return with the other brothers to stay. But these plans were rudely interrupted by the death of Papi Arturo only two weeks after returning to Puerto Rico to collect the rest of the family.

My mother had only a few grades of education and no trade. But with a faith firmly grounded in prayer and much determination, she found a job in a factory and finally saved enough pennies to send for her other sons. It was a happy reunion the day we were back together again, but little did we know that our struggles had just begun.

A few short years later, my mother was diagnosed with cancer. Surgery followed and we were told she would live no longer than a year, probably only six months.

We all tried to hold up our own post of duty, co-operating only for survival. During these hard days, my father and his wife moved to the New York City area bringing with them a strange new religion. We were neither impressed nor interested; our only interests being food (which was scarce), and the only real family bond —

mother's progress. By now, gambling, racism, gangs, my early curiosity in scientific inventions, girl friends, spiritualism, and personal popularity threatened to tear our family apart and leave us shredded irreparably.

In the midst of this chaos, a strange seed was planted in my heart. Music and show biz appeared to be the poor man's only escape from shame; and it assured him entrance into acceptance and good will. It bridged race, social class and intellectual attainment. It appeared to be a sure fix for all my woes.

At the age of thirteen, we formed our first group, "Donny and the Twilights." It fulfilled all my dreams and more. We had a manager, a contract, our own tailor-made suits, and our own car with our name on it. Fame came quickly and easily, and with it acceptance, popularity, and money.

The dream rolled on for a couple of years and then one morning reality shattered the delusions. Donny was found dead on his steps — overdosed on drugs. Momentarily, we all found ourselves disoriented. Donny had such a beautiful voice; so unusual we knew it would be next to impossible to replace him.

We had begun to learn to play instruments. I had chosen the bass guitar. Now it became necessary. We formed a larger group, a rock band named "The Vampires." Quickly we spiraled to monumental success. Named the "Band of the Week," our picture and name appeared on the famous Times Square building. Our fan club grew until no matter where we performed, a large motorcycle gang and many other persons were there.

I soon realized we had a very special rapport with the audiences. They were literally feeding at our table; tied by unseen chains to our every word — moving, crying, laughing, loving, despising, cooperating, rebelling — at our mere suggestion, whether that suggestion was enunciated or only felt in the music.

THE VAMPIRES, 1966. Louis Torres on front row, far right.

We knew we held them securely in our hands and we worked hard to bind them ever more securely under our sole influence. For the brief moments or hours of our performances we were the unchallenged lords and masters of all who were within our hearing. In every concert we worked our audiences through the whole gamut of earthy, human emotions. Truly artists, we painted our own pictures on the canvases of others' characters. Little did they think or realize we were painting with indelible colors, shaping their lives for the present and the future.

Believe it or not, it was the realization of this power, its use and abuse, that both captivated and frightened me. I began to realize that there was less and less "use" and more and more "abuse." My life — my personal character — was falling at an alarming speed. I thought, at the time, that this was the environment of our particular management and circumstances and I began to look for a way out.

I quit "The Vampires" and was invited to join "Bill Haley and the Comets." Believing it would be a better situation, I agreed to tour with them. Anticipation gave way to disillusionment. Immorality and drugs of every kind were even more prevalent, but oh so beguilingly clothed in aristocracy.

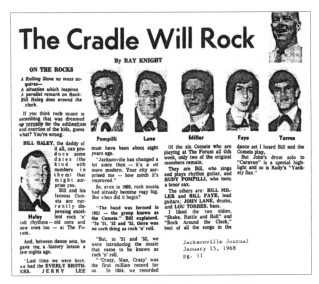

The Cradle Will Rock

By RAY KNIGHT

ON THE ROCKS

*A Rolling Stone no moss acquires—
A situation which inspires
A parallel remark on Rock:
Bill Haley does around the clock.*

If you think rock music is something that was dreamed up recently for the edification and exertion of the kids, guess what? You're wrong.

BILL HALEY, the daddy of it all, can produce some dates (the kind with numbers in them) that might surprise you. Bill and his famous Comets are currently dispensing excellent rock 'n' roll rhythms — old ones and new ones too — at The Forum.

And, between dance sets, he gave me a history lesson a few nights ago.

"Last time we were here, we had the EVERLY BROTHERS. JERRY LEE

must have been about eight years ago.

"Jacksonville has changed a lot since then — it's a lot more modern. Your city surprised me — how much it's improved."

So, even in 1960, rock music had already become very big. But when did it begin?

"The band was formed in 1951 — the group known as the Comets." Bill explained. "In '51, '52 and '53, there was no such thing as rock 'n' roll.

"But, in '51 and '52, we were introducing the music that came to be known as rock 'n' roll.

" 'Crazy, Man, Crazy' was the first million record for us . . . In 1954, we recorded

Pompilli   **Lane**   **Miller**   **Faye**   **Torres**

Of the six Comets who are playing at The Forum all this week, only two of the original members remain.

They are Bill, who sings and plays rhythm guitar, and RUDY POMPILLI, who toots a tenor sax.

The others are: BILL MILLER and BILL FAYE, lead guitars; JOHN LANE, drums, and LOU TORRES, bass.

I liked the two oldies, "Shake, Rattle and Roll" and "Rock Around the Clock," best of all the songs in the

dance set I heard Bill and the Comets play.

But John's drum solo to "Caravan" is a special highlight and so is Rudy's "Yackety Sax."

Jacksonville Journal
January 15, 1968
pg. 11

Bill Haley and the Comets. 1968.

Knowing my innermost heart, God had mercy and at the pinnacle of my success, at the age of twenty-one, through the conversion of two of my brothers to my father's strange religion, and an unusual experience in their church, God said, "Little Lou, you are serving yourself, setting yourself up as a god, ruining your own life and the lives of others. STOP! Stop, before you go too far. Accept Me as ruler of your life. Learn of Me… and you will find rest unto your soul." In one quick moment He showed me the depths of my degradation and the heights of His love. In fear and trembling I surrendered my life. Fear, because it was a giant step into the unknown. Trembling, because I was weak, a slave of my own god, music.

As God turned the world upside down by the early apostolic church, so He did to my life by His love and truth. The pages that follow are born from this experience and are an expression of my heart — a heart overstuffed with personal experiences and overflowing with thanksgiving for God's immeasureable mercy that would cause Him to "save to the uttermost" a man such as I.

Carol A. Torres — My Story

Being what many would consider a privileged child, I grew up with the blessings of a good home, a good education, and excellent music opportunities.

My only two wishes at the age of four were for a pet dog and a violin. I remember well the day I received my beloved Rusty. What a great dog he was; but a violin for such a tiny tot was not so easily supplied in those days.

After a patient two-year wait, my dream was finally realized when the family moved to Pacific Union College and lessons soon began. Due to an energetic teacher, my first full student recital was played at the end of the first year of lessons.

As I was a very shy child, but also deeply caring, I found in performance an avenue of expression for my love for people and life. Apparently this dimension of my performance was felt by the audiences as public appearances averaged two to three a week by the time I was nine. I also won my first scholarship, toured with a concert choir, and began playing in the college orchestra.

I loved to practice and maintained a practice schedule of three to five hours a day faithfully until a very unhappy experience with a teacher a number of years later dampened my desire to continue to excel, as doing so seemed to be misunderstood. I changed teachers a couple of times and finally began lessons with a lovely lady in the valley who, though not of my faith, was most respectful and helpful in arranging opportunities that did not militate against my convictions. Under her tutelage, I won numerous scholarships, awards, and performance opportunities with a number of symphonies.

After winning a scholarship to my choice of music conservatories, I opted instead to move to Loma Linda University, La Sierra Campus, to continue my music studies. A year later I entered college as a nursing major but was looking for a way to use my music in health care.

Sixteen-year-old Carol Reinke of Angwin just learned she is the local and state division winner of the National Federation of Music club auditions. The award means that Carol has the choice of a scholarship to either Eastmand School of Music, Rochester, N.Y., or Peabody School of Music, Baltimore, Md. Her decision will be announced shortly. 1967.

Music therapy was a relatively new field, but one that fascinated me. I took the opportunity in my psychology classes to research this area. I was surprised at the wealth of information available, but not drawn together or understood. A new hobby was introduced into my life — the study of the physiological effects of music.

After my marriage to Louie, I taught music in New York and performed with the Long Island Symphony, finally as its concert master. Again, I was offered very appealing scholarships for private lessons with some of the nation's finest, and also to complete my music degree at the State University of New York, Stonybrook Conservatory of Music. Because I was also offered an assistant professorship at the University, I found the offer tempting.

But inner loyalties to a deeper conviction of service moved me back to California where my husband studied for the ministry and where I continued to teach music.

I later completed a degree in Music Performance, a degree in Elementary Education, as well as much study in Health Education. The work reflected in the pages of this book is only one special interest among many. But my conviction is that the question of music may be far more pertinent to the personal victory of God's people than most of us even dream possible.

Carol and Louis: Performing for the international television program, *Ayer, Hoy y Mañana*. 1974.

Chapter I

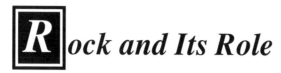

R ock and Its Role

Hardly had the world finished "licking its wounds" after World War I, when news arrived of the German armies' terrible conquests in Europe. People's dreams were dashed, as city after city fell to Hitler. Utter discouragement paralyzed millions as they realized the hopelessness of their situation. The European nations needed help but the world was desperately divided in its worries, for half a world away, Japan was also steadily advancing its borders through brutal conquest at an alarming speed.

In between these two terrible fronts sat the United States of America, still bruised and broken, hoping against hope not to have to get involved. After all, argued many, it wasn't their argument, not their war, not their problem and thus should not require their sacrifice — the blood of their sons, their brothers, their fathers.

Others reasoned differently. What if, without U.S. aid, the "Allied" countries around the world fell to the "Axis" countries? Who then would help defend U.S. soil should the Axis powers, charged by their great successes, decide to finish the job by attacking the United States of America? Not a few shared this latter concern, including the President. But try as he would, his great country would not be united in its commitment to war.

December 1941 would be a month to change all that. United States intelligences had been working hard to understand the secret code of the Axis armies. On December 4, President Roosevelt received word that the code had been

1

broken and that the Japanese were planning to attack U.S. positions in the Hawaiian Islands.

The normal reaction would be to prepare to strike back, but President Roosevelt thought better. Perhaps his forces in the islands were in a good enough state of preparedness that a surprise attack would not be too devastating; besides, if they sent word to prepare, the Axis armies would know that they now understood the secret code and would then change it, making the U.S. wait in "darkness" again till the new code could be broken. There was also the good possibility that just such an attack was what was needed to bring the American public together, unified in a common goal.

For such reasons the President's mind was made up: He would not breathe a word of his knowledge to anyone till tragedy had struck. And strike it did, only three days later.

December 7 dawned. It was a beautifully clear morning in the Islands. Because of festivities and honors bestowed the night before, the captain of the U.S.S. Arizona allowed his men a rare privilege of sleeping in. Others were about their usual duties for a Sunday morning. An open air Mass was being held with about 200 men in attendance. Then suddenly over the mountain range immediately behind Pearl Harbor, the Japanese bombers came in relentless waves. The men of the U.S.S. Arizona — more than a thousand of them — suffered a short but tragic nightmare, then slept on. The two hour "surprise" attack was executed much more brilliantly than the President had expected and it cost the United States 18 ships, 170 planes, and about 3700 lives. The very next day, the U.S. Congress declared war.

Americans were stirred to action. In the Islands, volunteers worked around the clock to clean up, patch up, and put back into action, the base and its equipment, including many ships and planes. In the homeland, no division now existed. All were of one mind. Fight, and fight to the end. Win? Yes, we will! Songs of victory and courage sprang up everywhere and the United States moved together toward a common goal. World War II soldiers returned home as heroes and with great dignity. Though the losses were great, the overall experience of victory was sweet.

A little over a decade later, a little squabble started in Viet Nam. A small country with big problems — or so it seemed. Big brother, U.S.A., was going to solve those problems, gently, but in short order. Instead, they landed in quicksand — the more the U.S.A did, the more deeply they became involved. Again the nation was divided, so presidents tried the "Roosevelt tactic," hoping that by shocking the Americans by the aggressive acts committed against her they could rally the people one more time to a concerted effort.

In place of a rally, there were riots.

In place of volunteers, there were defectors by the thousands.

In place of patriotism, there were flag burnings.

Anti U.S. government sentiments spread quickly to nations around the globe. No matter how they (the government) used the media, how they lobbied, there was no point of turning back; no way of salvation. Where the cry "Remember Pearl Harbor" sparked pride and dignity and where it stirred the inner soul to patriotism, "Remember Viet Nam" chimed shame and disgrace, and even today may spawn shock waves of rebellion.

Was this all by chance? Was it simply that one war was justifiable, the other not? I am sure that in the minds of many this is the most probable answer. But how then do you explain a "dove" mentality that is violent and abusive—showing such disregard for life and property as was evidenced in the anti-war riots and revolutions; and even now in the defacing of the monument to the memory of the dead or missing Viet Nam soldiers? What made the difference? I am sure there are many factors, variables if you please, but as we carefully studied the society of the United States of America during this time, we were particularly impressed by the way Americans chose what they were going to listen to. What many chose was not their leaders — their representatives — but rather a very "different tune."

Come with us in your minds as we lead you through those times and as we "listen" — in a brief way — to the "tunes" of a new generation.

A New Tune

The time is the fifties. Radios are in nearly every home. Television is the "new kid on the block." Sounds are being heard all over America that are strange to the average listener. It seems as though the "dens of iniquity," so religiously kept to their "districts," are suddenly bursting their seams; overflowing their confines. We hear the raucous voice of Bill Haley and his Comets belting out their "Rock Around the Clock" — which since has been recognized as the first international rock hit. We hear Elvis Presley, the first solo rock star, drawling his "You Ain't Nothing But A Hound Dog."

Radio producers took note and were quick to realize that the promotion of this new music could well be their only hope for recapturing their audiences from television. Disc jockeys became powerful people in the promotion of "stars" and as role models for the young and reckless.

Within just a few years the powerful medium of music as a sculpturing force on the face of America became recognized and exploited. Radical voices seized the opportunity. The early sixties found the rock enthusiast in sweet-smelling, smoke-filled coliseums or open air gatherings. The attraction? A rather crude looking (to us then) trio, Peter, Paul, and Mary. Their message? The uselessness of war; the hypocrisy of national authority; the injustices of intrusions into private lives through the draft and taxes; the hypocrisy of a plastic society; and the need for peace and love. Truth to a large degree; but truth wrapped in cynicism and disaffection. Their medium of communication was a folkstyle music, later mingled with soft rock. But the power of their medium mixed with the poison of their attitude made its mark, and their voices became a mighty swell.

To this swell, Bob Dylan, "the conscience of the rock generation,"[1] joined his voice as well as his uncanny ability to transform "the aimless rebellion and anger inherent in rock and roll into a socially-directed impulse toward action…"[2] The minds of the young were rocking and reeling from stem to stern, between restraint and abandonment, between norms and anarchy.

Soon, Beatlemania swept the nation. To young and old alike they were shocking; but to the young the shock became an addiction, taking the usual course of needing added potency over time to keep up the high. The first songs seemed so innocent: "I Want to Hold Your Hand," "Yesterday" and "Can't Buy Me Love." Soon, however, it was evident that we were on a musical bridge, the other end of which was definitely connected to a different culture and lifestyle — a different code of ethics. "Lucy In the Skies With Diamonds" (LSD) and "Yellow Submarine" led to other songs and record covers that went from bad to worse so quickly that the public, as a whole, recoiled and in many instances boycotted.

But never mind, "…they wrote and sang songs. We turned it into politics and philosophy and a road map to another way of life."[3] So there were lots of voices ready to pick up the pieces and carry the ball into the end-zone. Or at least we thought then it was the "end zone," for rock seemed to have gone as far as it could. "Once captured by the rock beat, you moved in a whole new way. You talked in a new way, once you absorbed those strangulated, elliptical lyrics. You sang in a new way. You heard in a new way — through feet and hands, through pores in the skin, not just through your ears. The electronic density of the sound transcended sheer volume and assumed mass, became a multi-sensory bombardment, a bath of sound in a semi-solid medium, an enveloping sensation like floating in warm jelly, a womb of music."[4]

Many in this "womb" expressed themselves in violent acts for which the '60s became famous. With messages of discontent the common fare for millions of young people, is it any wonder that this period became known for drugs, rebellion, riots, defections, "flower children," sex, venereal disease epidemics, waves of street violence, new highs in divorce and shattered homes and lives? Some have observed that not one rally nor one riot during this period took place that did not do so to the tune or chant of a theme from one of the current rock songs. Every norm was challenged, every virtue demeaned. Every authority embarrassed. Truly, in the words of the former Soviet diplomat, Arhady Schevchenko, "The Viet Nam war would be won not in Viet Nam but in the streets of America."[5] And so it was. Finally, all that was left was chaos, rack and ruin. The decade ended in terrible violence.

Had rebellion continued in its then level of savagery, it would have soon suffered self-destruction. Many hoped it would; many, that is, who did not find themselves with a beloved son or daughter, the pride and joy of their hearts, reeling in the violent circles of the social mayhem.

As time's clock struck the '70s, the destructive tide turned in another unexpected direction. A young man by the name of Vince Furnier, having spent much time watching television, felt he knew what the world wanted. At a seance he made a pact with the Devil. He would take on the name of a 17th century witch in exchange for the Devil's blessings. He launched a career as a rock musician, soon being known for his mock executions of babies. When this grew old, he started using live chickens, pulling their legs and heads off and throwing their parts into the crowd. Ugly? Yes — disgusting; but for some, not enough. Take for example, "Cold Ethyl," a song praising the virtues of sex with the dead; or another one of his famous songs, "I Love The Dead." This is sung to the erotic behavior suggested, with what appears to be a real corpse on stage.

Who is this Vince Furnier? Actually, he is a son of a minister; now he is known as Alice Cooper.

Other groups zeroed in on Satanism, performing actual levitations during concerts.

A Gallup poll taken in the early eighties found that the three most popular groups of the youth of America were groups whose primary thrust was just such divergent behavior. Such trends prompted Kingsbury Smith, editor of the Hearst newspaper, to make this observation: "What can parents expect during this decade (the '80s) as rock music advocates sadism, masochism, incest, necrophilia, homosexuality, bestiality, rape and violence in addition to the ever-present rebellion, drug abuse and promiscuity? The obvious answer is stupefying."[6]

Did the '80s live up to the expectations? The music, our society's closest companion, has continued to pound out the same messages in ever lessening shame. No prophet of doom, consequently, has had to experience the "Jonah syndrome" of anger or embarrassment for their prophecies of destruction and degeneration not coming true.

Take drugs for example. During the years 1981-85, there was an 1100% increase in drug-related emergencies. In Dallas, during the first six months of 1986, there were more drug related emergencies in one hospital than there had been in all of the hospitals in Dallas for the entire previous year. "Crack" is completely ruling many neighborhoods and cities. The entire economy of some cities is dependent on drug traffic. Some states are also very dependent on drug traffic for economic stability.

The number of homosexuals is increasing with alarming rapidity — quickly becoming respectable in many circles — and without question one of the strongest and most successful lobbies in Congress.

Promiscuity and its related diseases are rampant. The awareness of AIDS suppressed the spread of sexually transmitted diseases for a short time until it was discovered that

AIDS was spreading equally as fast or faster in drug users. Those not using drugs slipped back into old practices, and the consequences? — all venereal diseases, including AIDS, are spreading in "wildfire" epidemic proportions.

Crime is up. Suicide is spreading very fast. Masochism, sadism, incest, and necrophilia are much, much, more common. Lawlessness is the norm. Only one thing is down, way down, and that is literacy!

Yes, these are the "tunes" to which America was listening — the tunes of the rebellious and the deviant. And like it or not, the behavior of millions has followed suit.

Is This Fair?

We have stated rather unequivocally that we believe music has a strong influence on the direction — the mentality and morality — of society. The question must then be asked honestly: Is this a fair assessment?

Listen to what two prominent philosophers have said about music. "Emotions of any kind are produced by melody and rhythm. . . Music has the power to form character. . . the manner of its arrangement being so important that the various modes may be distinguished by their effects on character. One, for example, working in the direction of melancholy, another of effeminacy; one encouraging abandonment, another self-control, another enthusiasm; and so on through the series."[7] "When modes of music change, the fundamental laws of the state always change with them (for) this spirit of license, finding a home, imperceptibly penetrates into manners and customs; whence, issuing with greater force, it invades contracts between man and man, and from contracts goes on to laws and constitutions, in utter recklessness, ending at last, by an overthrow of all rights, private as well as public."[8]

The men who wrote these two philosophical observations are Aristotle and Plato, writing between 300 to 400 years before Christ. But what do more contemporary critics say?

8

Howard Hanson, a prominent composer formerly with the Eastman School of Music, states: "Music is a curiously subtle art with innumerable, varying emotional connotations. It is made up of many ingredients and, according to the proportions of these components, it can be soothing or invigorating, ennobling or vulgarizing, philosophical or orgiastic. It has powers for evil as well as for good."[9] "It is no surprise then," states an encyclopedia, "to find that philosophers and commentators have stressed its dual influence on the character of men. Music may be a force for good; evoking that which is spiritual, patriotic, noble, or ethical. It may be a force for evil, exciting the merely physical and lascivious, and may be subversive of moral behavior."[10]

Another composer and conductor, Dimitri Tiomkin, shares his views. "The fact that music can both excite and incite has been known from time immemorial. That was perhaps its chief function in prehistory and it remains so in the primitive societies which still exist in the far reaches of the world. In civilized countries, music became more and more a means of communicating pleasurable emotions, not creating havoc. Now in our popular music, at least, we seem to be reverting to savagery. . . and youngsters who listen constantly to this sort of sound are thrust into turmoil. They are no longer relaxed, normal kids."[11]

A pro-rock writer and editor continues: "In this sense, the Beatles are part of a chain: a) the Beatles opened up rock; b) rock changed the culture; c) the culture changed us."[12]

We could continue indefinitely for this is a widely believed and accepted concept. Music does affect society. Music **alone** affects. Lyrics only serve to make that effect more explicit, or, as in some cases, more confusing. The late Jimmy Hendrix said, "You can hypnotize people with music and when they get at their weakest point, you can preach into their subconscious minds what you want to say."[13]

Would to God, this was only true outside the confines of

our church community. But no, the wrong use of this medium of music, the common denominator of rebellion against norms, authority, and God Himself, regardless of social class, color, or creed, has found its way into our homes, our schools; yes, even our churches.

1. William J. Schafer, *Rock Music* (Augsburg Publishing House, 1972), p. 34.
2. Ibid, p. 29.
3. Janet Podell, *The Reference Shelf — Rock Music in America* (H W. Wilson Company, New York, 1987), p. 44.
4. Schafer, p. 55.
5. American Broadcasting Company, Documentary, "1945 to 1985," Narrated by Peter Jennings and Ted Koppel.
6. *Seattle Post-Intelligencer,* April 12, 1980, p. 8B.
7. Aristotle, *Politics,* 1339a, b.
8. Plato, *Republic,* bk. IV, p. 425.
9. Howard Hanson, "A Musician's Point of View Toward Emotional Expression," *American Journal of Psychiatry,* Vol. 99, p. 317.
10. "Music," *Collier Encyclopedia* (1965), Vol. 17, p. 2.
11. *Los Angeles Herald-Examiner,* August 8, 1965, p. 9J.
12. Podell, p. 48.
13. Jimmy Hendrix, *Life Magazine,* October 3, 1969, p. 4.

 hythm Rules

God Created Harmony

As God planned this marvelous universe which was to be the playground of mankind, He was thinking in terms of eternity: Eternal happiness, eternal intrigue, eternal peace, eternal harmony. From the minutest particle to the most colossal, detail, glorious detail, was attended to and built into all that God created. But not one detail, however apparently insignificant, was intended to stand alone but to be part of a whole. Every element was for the benefit of something else; always giving and thus always receiving. Cycles were within cycles and systems within systems. A "wheel within a wheel": A Divine atmosphere of harmonious rhythms.

In our relatively small world, we never cease to be amazed by the intricacies and sensitive balance of our ecological systems. Nor do we cease to fear for the jeopardy into which we have placed our very survival as a result of our carelessness and indifference to just such harmony.

Man's Harmony Based on Rhythm

This same balance, this same interrelationship and interdependence, cycles and rhythms, is very much apparent in the human body as well. "We are essentially rhythmic creatures. Everything from the cycle of our brain waves to the pumping of our heart, our digestive cycle, sleep cycle — all work in rhythms. We're a mass of cycles piled one on top of another, so we're clearly organized both to generate and respond to rhythmic phenomena."[1]

Each one of us has a personal rhythmic tempo that we exhibit in our speech, gestures and gait ranging from 60 to 120 beats per minute, with the majority of us clustered between 70 and 80 beats per minute. Interestingly, we tend to be most compatible with those whose rhythmic tempo is close to our own, a fact not too surprising when you stop to think of one's attitude toward people we view as being on the "fast track" or "a little slow."[2] *Carol Douglas, A Beat Too Slow*

These "rhythmic or cyclic phenomena, characteristic of nature, are observed on all levels of biological organization. Within an organism, many physiological processes occur which are not only conspicuously rhythmical but also self-reinforcing and necessary for survival, such as brain activity, heart beat and pulse rate. All of these endogenous rhythms are synchronized with other cellular activities and are harmonic with body functioning."[3]

Disharmony Causes "Dis-ease"

The problems that arise from interfering with these cycles and rhythms of the body are very well known to medicine. "If an organism is the target of excessive, disharmonic stimuli, a number of stress mechanisms, involving both endocrine and neural feedback, are subsequently evoked by the body. If these defensive actions become overburdened, then natural harmonic biological rhythms are disrupted, resulting in systemic disharmony and possibly even breakdown. If homeostasis cannot be attained then the stress condition can manifest itself in pathological disorders. In fact, fluctuations and disturbances in pre-existing body rhythms have been correlated with many diseases like diabetes, renal and hepatic disorders, ulcers, cancer and circulatory abnormalities (Reimann, 1963).

"Since most regulatory mechanisms are neural in origin,

12

it is not surprising that many pathological alterations could also occur in neuronal structures. In the case of brain cells, this 'disordering' can manifest itself not only in the physical state of neurons but also in the harmony of their functioning, as well. Consequently, the behavior of the organism may become seriously affected."[4]   Neurol Plastisity of MUS

Perhaps the most common and obvious expressions of this "disordering" process are the results of disrupting the sleep cycle. We are all very familiar with the results of such disruptions on children and the varying degrees of unpleasant behavior that follows. Not as common and well known are the terrible results of such disruptions used as torture against prisoners of war. Such graphic results serve to remind us that no one law of our being stands alone or can be considered inconsequential. Greater respect must be shown to the "total picture" surrounding mankind; his being, his world, his universe.

Music — Part of Creation

Just as there are natural laws that govern the physiology of our bodies and minds, so there are natural laws that govern music. These principles of good music have been established by careful observation and more recently, scientific study.

Believing that the "laws" of structure were arbitrarily imposed by men of less than current understanding, man, in the music world, as in many other disciplines, has tried to rearrange these laws for "special effects" or create new laws with no bonds or similarities to the "old."

One reason for these detours might be found in the fact that, to many, the laws of music have seemed to be the results of mere preference. Another reason doubtless stems from the fact that "Western" music appears to be dominated by the "Christian mind" as it differs so widely from styles used by the non-Christian societies of the world, even today. Any person, not wanting to be subject to Christian influences or wanting to prove "independent thinking," would very naturally move

13

away from the product of a Judeo-Christian culture. A third reason that comes to mind is that, until very recently, the relationship of music to the health of society and our own personal health has largely been ignored, even considered nonexistent by most. Tastes in music have long been proclaimed to be merely a matter of personal choice thus leaving the field open for experimentation.

Music Is Rhythm

Music is made by combining and balancing five basic elements. These are (1) MELODY — tones arranged to make a tune; (2) TONE COLOR — the quality of the sounds produced by instruments or the voice; (3) HARMONY — the stacking of tones so as to create chords; (4) RHYTHM — a specific allotment of time given to a note or syllable in verse and the time meter of a composition of music; and (5) TEMPO — how fast or slow the rhythm is to be played or sung.

Though not obvious to the casual observer, **all these elements consist of rhythmic vibrations and/or rhythmic cycles**. Tones are created by specific vibrations, the number of which determines the pitch and intonation of each tone. All sounds are vibrations. The universal "A" for example, vibrates 440 times per second. (With a universal music standard, it becomes conveniently easy to share music and players worldwide.) Tone color is determined by the vibration of overtones as well as the presence or absence of surface sounds, sympathetic vibrations, and breath or mechanical sounds. These later sounds are often referred to as noise, or "dirty" sounds.

Harmony, of course, falls into the same category as it is simply the stacking of these vibrations. If the vibrations of these intervals, or chords, create "clean" sounds (the absence of secondary beats that have a slightly distorting effect on the pitch) we call the harmony "consonate." Examples of such

14

consonate chords are thirds, fourths, fifths, and sixths. The perfect fourth and perfect fifth as well as a perfect octave comprise the most consonate sounds because the vibrations of their various tones together create no secondary beats. The third and sixth create a very slight secondary beat, not audible to most ears. However, the secondary beats created by a second or seventh are noticeable, even to the untrained ear. These latter chords, or intervals, are referred to as being "dissonant." "Consonances provide stability and repose, while dissonances produce tension and motion by 'pulling' toward a resolution in a consonance."[5] For the purpose of our overall discussion, consonance will be referred to as "harmonic" and dissonance as "disharmonic."

The element of rhythm in music is primarily cyclic in nature, thus creating the "time meter." There are two basic arrangements upon which all early time meters were based: the two/four family (of which the 4/4 time signature is most common); and the three/four family. In the 4/4 cycle, the natural emphasis (or accents) fall on the one (the primary accent) and three (the secondary accent) counts of the measure. In the 3/4 meter, the primary accent is on the one count and the secondary accent is on the three count as a preparatory beat leading to the first count of the following measure. In most cases, the secondary accent is not very noticeable. As insignificant as these accents seem, right here begins most of the problems with music's effect being negative. "Swing" music began by simply moving these accents to the "unnatural" position of the second and fourth beats in a 4/4 meter. This led to syncopation, polysyncopation, and polyrhythms, of which we will speak more later.

Because there is a "right" and "wrong" use of all of these elements, a succinct division might be helpful. For this reason, a list of these elements plus two elements of performance may be found in the first column of the following page. The second column is the "harmonic" use of the element in brief, and the third column is the "disharmonic" use of the element, again in brief. In no way is this chart to be viewed as complete, but rather a very brief listing of guidelines. (For further discussion, see the Appendix on page 50.)

Integration of Man and Music

We have discussed the marvelous relationship that exists in God's universe between the multitudinous rhythms and cycles of nature. We have noted that the human body also functions at its optimum when its various rhythmic cycles can operate in perfect balance and harmony. We then discovered that music is composed of rhythmic vibrations and cycles, the arrangement of which creates either consonance (harmony) or dissonance (disharmony). Now we face the challenge of achieving an harmonic relationship between the rhythms of music and rhythms of the human body, as well as understanding the "whys" of such harmony. (See following page.)

In our search, we will be looking at 1) the effect of harmonic and disharmonic music on the functions of the body; 2) the effect of harmonic and disharmonic music on human behavior; and 3) the effect of harmonic and disharmonic music on the structure of the body and mind.

"In this regard we define any influence and its causative agent as harmonic (H) if experimental evidence bears out that it enhances, sustains, or is otherwise constructive to the normal structure and functioning of the organism or part thereof, and disharmonic (D) if it suppresses, restrains, or is otherwise destructive to the normal structure and functioning of the organism or part thereof."[6]

Music's Power to Penetrate

How is it that music enters and transmits its messages and influence throughout the body? Most everyone understands the most basic processes of the ear — how sound waves (vibrations), acting upon the ear drum are transformed to

16

Chart 1

ELEMENTS OF MUSIC AND PERFORMANCE		
Element of Music	**Harmonic Use**	**Disharmonic Use**
Melody	Pleasing Melody (can stand alone)	Little or No Melody (needs help)
Tone Color	Pleasant & Clear	Harsh, Dirty
Harmony	Clean, Harmonious Chords, Correct Intonation	Cluttered, Lots of Dissonant Chords, Incorrect Intonation (Sloppy)
Rhythm	Clustered About and Fully Sympathetic to Main Beat: Variety	Frequent or Perpetual Syncopation or Polyrhythms; Monotonous
Tempo	Between 60 & 120 (mostly 70-80) Beats Per Minute & Phrased	Too Slow or Too Fast
Words	Biblically Sound; Positive	Repetitious; Sentimental; Biblically Unsound
Presentation	Natural, Unaffected; From the Heart	Dramatic

17

chemical and nerve impulses which register in our minds the different qualities of the sounds we are hearing. What many do not know is that the "roots of the auditory nerves — the nerves of the ear — are more widely distributed and have more extensive connections than those of any other nerves in the body. . . (Due to this extensive networking) there is scarcely a function of the body which may not be affected by the pulsations and harmonic combinations of musical tones."[7] *Music For Your Health*

This means that "music attacks the nervous system directly. . . ."[8] Additionally, "music, which does not depend upon the master brain (centers of reason) to gain entrance into the organism, can still arouse by way of the thalamus — the relay station of all emotions — sensations and feelings. Once a stimulus has been able to reach the thalamus, the master brain is automatically invaded. . ."[9] The significance of these statements lies in the revelation that music, though bypassing the centers of judgment, affects these centers by way of the emotional responses elicited by the music through the thalamus. Other researchers emphasize the effects of music on the nervous system by stressing the influence of the auditory pathways on the autonomic nervous system.[10] Though emphasis from research to research varies, the point remains the same: auditory stimuli directly affects the nervous system and that effect is systemic.

1. Functional Stressors

What then, are some of the areas within which one might observe functional changes? Probably the two most important areas would be a) the nerve or message pathways of the body and b) the emotional changes brought about by the thalamus. Secondary to these would be processes directly or indirectly affected by a) and b) above such as heart rate, respiration, blood pressure, digestion, hormonal balance and swings, electrolyte balance, as well as emotions, moods and attitudes.[11] (Note Chart 3 on page 30.)

18

Exposure to "harmonic" music reinforces the rhythmic cycles of the body; balancing processes, synchronizing nerve messages, bringing moods and emotions into a rest state of homeostasis, as well as enhancing coordination (to be discussed later). Exposure to "disharmonic" music—whether it be the "tension" caused by dissonance and "noise" or the unnatural swings of misplaced rhythmical accents, syncopation, and polyrhythms, or inappropriate tempo — can result in a variety of changes including: an altered heart rate with its corresponding change in blood pressure; an overstimulation of hormones (especially the opiates or endorphins) causing an altered state of consciousness from mere exhilaration on one end of the spectrum to unconsciousness on the other; and improper digestion.

So deep seated is our body's association with certain elements of music that "short of numbing the entire brain, neurologists have been unable to suppress rhythmic ability. Doping either side of the brain, or many regions at once, still leaves the patient able to count or clap in time."[12]

"In ancient as well as modern civilization, music has helped to synchronize the movements of workers. In fact, many folk songs originated in this way. Of course, the music also helped to relieve the monotony of their toil."[13] Experiments in offices and industries have led to the conclusion that the rhythm of the music effects the precision or accuracy of the work. "Specially selected music increases the working capacity of the muscles. At the same time, the tempo of the movements of the worker changes with the change of the musical tempo. It is as if the music determines a good rapid rhythm of movement."[14] But, for example, "when the rhythm is contrary to the speed of typewriting, there (is) a decrease in accuracy."[15]

This same loss of coordination can be experienced by mixing rhythmic stimuli such as a strobe light pulsating at a different and non-synchronized rate of speed from the music of the band. Under such circumstances, movements become erratic and halting.

The secret behind this apparent manipulation is that "sound vibrations acting upon and through the nervous system give shocks in rhythmical sequence to the muscles, which cause them to contract and set our arms and hands, legs and feet in motion. On account of this automatic muscular reaction, many people make some movement when hearing music; for them to remain motionless would require conscious muscular restraint."[16] It is obvious then that the body responds to the stimuli without a conscious or unconscious judgement as to whether or not the incoming rhythm is compatible with its own functions.

Even casual observance bears out the veracity of these statements. Consider such ordinary activities as dancing and marching. While the music is playing or the march beat is being counted aloud, all can move in perfect synchronization. But within seconds of the cessation of such rhythmic stimuli, such harmony soon disappears. Each begins to move to the beat of their own internal clockwork, few of which are going to be exactly the same.

How Far Is Too Far?

It is obvious then that a) the body is deeply rhythmical and that b) each individual has his own clock ticking out his own rhythm of homeostasis. But it is also just as obvious that c) these individual rhythms may be voluntarily submitted or simply overridden by outside rhythmic stimuli. If we can alter the body's natural rhythmic swings simply by exposing it to outside stimuli that differ in rhythm and tempo from its own, and we can, the question then is; to what extent is this overriding process safe?

An article concerned with this very question has this to say: "Man is essentially a rhythmical being. . . There is rhythm in respiration, heart beat, speech, gait, etc. The cerebral hemispheres are in a perpetual state of rhythmical swing day and night. **To maintain a sense of well-being and integration,**

20

it is essential that man is not subjected too much to any rhythms not in accord with his own natural bodily rhythms." (Emphasis supplied.)[17] Most research seems to point to this one factor — compatibility between the rhythms (or beats) of the music and rhythms of the body — as the most influential in the success or failure of harmonically integrating man and music. If the tempo of the music is faster than the normal tempo of the body, the consequences are generally a quickening and over-stimulation of the body processes. Likewise, the opposite is true of a very slow-tempoed music. Such results have led some to conclude that "tempo may be the most important factor for our hearts and our heads. Our hearts normally beat 70 to 80 times per minute. Most Western music is set (coincidentally?) to this tempo."[18]

So, how far out of sinc is too far? Any pull or push that causes the body to have to fight for homeostasis is a "pull or push" too far. Naturally, the results, immediate or lasting, depend on the extent of exposure, the extent of deviation from the norm, as well as one's personal strength and level of resistance to foreign states of being. This is true of any species within the animal kingdom and, of course, we know it to be true of the inanimate world of machines and appliances: too little power input and it doesn't work, too much and you "fry" the controls.

2. How Am I Behaving?

In a healthy state of balance mentally, physically, and emotionally, one can expect, and usually find, a person's processes of judgement and decisions to also be balanced, calm, and under control. We say they are "well adjusted." Little traumas don't move them far away from their smooth ride. Others observe them and think that they are "so even." We like this characteristic in leadership because it gives a real sense of stability and security. Harmonic music reinforces this state of balance.

21

The flip side of this, however, is a very different picture. Remember that one of the functional changes with disharmonic music is the release of too-high doses of opiates and other hormones. This creates an overcharged emotional state. Some of these emotional traumas come to us in a way that we are able to recognize easily such as the fear that we experience at the scene of an accident or in a fire, or some other life-threatening situation. We can feel our hearts pounding; we sense the cold sweat and we literally fight with ourselves to keep calm, cool, and collected. If we should lose control, if our body is unable to bring us back to a state of homeostasis, we might do any number of very foolish things or we may slip into an unconscious state of shock.

But other emotional "highs" steal up on us very much unnoticed. Perhaps the most classic example of this is the emotional high of sentimental love — a state so obvious to everyone else and so totally unobserved by the person(s) involved. In this condition, one can be given every logic, spared no words or evidences, bribed, beaten, and flogged, but nine times out of ten (at least) will continue as is, till the emotional high burns out. Judgement is impaired, important decisions are boggled, and improper behavior follows. In fact, the most obvious evidence of emotional disturbance is altered behavior.[19]

In early literature, the processes in which the body engages to maintain homeostasis of the emotions is referred to as the inhibitory and excitatory processes. Very simply, the inhibitors can be likened to the brakes of a car and the excitors to the gas. When one applies both the gas and the brakes at the same time, the car cannot move ahead smoothly. One or the other process gives way, causing the car to halt or speed away out of control. Such an emotional state is simply referred to as "neurosis." We all quickly associate this word with deviant behavior—extreme introversion, despondency, and depression, to nervousness, wild unpredictable behavior and extreme aggression. Such a state can also cause hyperactivity, heightened mob instinct, abnormal fears, bad attitudes, and lethargic or lazy behavior, as well as impaired memory and learning processes.

This last fact is what has educators and learning/memory specialists all excited. When it was discovered that rock music is disharmonic, and that it causes behavior disorders, including problems with learning and memory, a very quick mandate spread around—"Don't study while listening to rock music."[20] Many, realizing that this is the only kind of music most people listen to, have gone so far as to instruct would-be learners to not study to music, period.[21]

So disorders caused by disharmonic music can range from "the intoxication of the dance"[22] to wild frenzies — even seizures[23]; from suicide to violent aggression. Whether the unbalancing of the mind is little or great, the judgement impaired slightly or grossly, the behavior altered briefly or continually, the fact is that while in a state of emotional imbalance, judgement cannot be trusted, thus behavior also slips out of sync.

But please remember, impaired judgement and improper behavior might be obvious to the individual affected but more often than not, they are the last to realize it. There they are, out of balance, out of sync, out of harmony — not necessarily with others in their society, but within themselves, with nature, and unfortunately, with the God of creation.

Let's briefly review what we have learned so far and tie up any loose ends.
1. Music affects society. This effect may be either uplifting (positive), or degrading (negative).
2. All of God's creation is harmonious and rhythmical.
3. Man is essentially a rhythmical being.
4. Every component of music is rhythmical.

5. Music affects man's rhythmic processes directly through the nervous system, bypassing the higher centers of reason and judgement via the auditory nerves.

6. Music directly affects the autonomic nervous system thus having the potential to affect all of its systems.

7. a. Man has a balance system — the inhibitory and excitatory process — which is both directly and indirectly affected by negative stress stimuli which includes any rhythmical or cyclic disruption as is experienced by disharmonic musical sounds.

   b. When this process becomes unbalanced, and the body cannot correct the imbalance quite promptly, behavior disorders result such as hyperactivity, aggressiveness, impaired judgement, heightened mob instinct, impaired memory and learning processes, breakdowns in health, abnormal fears, bad attitudes, and lethargic or lazy behavior, to name a few.

8. These facts apply to every human being regardless of ethnic origin or cultural background. (Because music bypasses the higher centers of reason and judgement, these effects are universal to mankind.[24] In fact, to all mammalians.) The question may be raised here: Can man, through the employment of his higher centers alter these effects? The answer is: To a certain extent, yes. **But only while listening to the music critically.**[25]

24

3. Structural Breakdown

For our discussion of structural changes brought about by disharmonic music I want to share a research project completed in 1988 that speaks eloquently to the issue.

Two researchers, Dr. Schreckenberg, a neurologist, and Dr. Bird, a physicist, wanted to discover if there would be any effect and, if so, what the effect might be, of harmonic and disharmonic music on neuronal mechanisms of the brain. Because no previous studies had been done, to their knowledge, that established what kind of music was harmonic (according to the definition found on pages 15 to 17) and what kind of music was disharmonic, they found it necessary to carry out preliminary studies. These preliminary laboratory studies "established that classical musical stimuli with synchronized component rhythmic patterns provided an 'harmonic' sound environment, and that musical stimuli with non-synchronized component rhythms (typical of the polyrhythms of African music and the syncopation of Western rock 'n' roll) provided a 'disharmonic' sound environment."[26]

The Process:

Thirty-six mice were divided at birth into three categories: (C) the control group, (H) the harmonic group (those exposed to the harmonic music), and (D) the disharmonic group (those exposed to disharmonic music). For two months the (H) and (D) groups were exposed, night and day, to their respective music, maintained at a sound level of 80-85 decibels. The (C) group was kept in a relatively quiet room at 75 decibels. The environments were in all other ways identical.

After these two months of exposure, 12 mice, four from each group, were sacrificed and their brains properly prepared and frozen for later study and comparisons with what would be the older mice by the time all had been sacrificed for study.

The other 24 mice were exposed to three weeks of maze "training." Then they were given three weeks of rest during which time no testing or maze reinforcement occurred. This was followed by a three week post latency period during which the mice were retested to establish the degree of learning and retention. Throughout this process, behavior changes and discrepancies were carefully noted. At the completion of the maze training, these 24 mice were sacrificed and their brains were studied along with the previous 12.

The Results:
1. The (C) and (H) groups were very similar, no significant differences appeared.
2. The (D) group showed the following changes:

    a. Excess branching of the Neuronal dendrites. (Notice Chart 2, p. 29.)

    b. Significant increases in mRNA (messenger Ribonucleic acid).

    c. Significant decreases in learning retention or memory.

    d. Hyperactivity.

    e. Aggression (during the three month preliminary testing, some mice resorted to cannibalism. Established by talking to Dr. Bird.)

    f. Lethargy and inattentiveness.

This all translates into two simple phrases we can all understand: The disharmonic music causes 1) brain nerve damage and 2) behavior degradation.[27]

The Conclusion

Yes, rhythm rules. Our only choice in the matter is to what rhythms we will expose ourselves; to the rhythms of harmony, or to the rhythms that disturb harmony? Contrary to what many of us have previously believed, there truly is no middle road with music. It either enhances the Creator's design and nature's pull "toward optimum (harmonic) balance"[28] or it interferes with the balance so necessary for our health mentally, physically, emotionally, and spiritually. It is either uplifting or degrading. May our choice ever be to cooperate with our God that His desire for our lives might be realized: "That (we) might have life and have it more abundantly!"[29]

---

1. Carole Douglis, "The Beat Goes On," *Psychology Today*, November 1987, p. 42.
2. Ibid., pp. 37-42.
3. Gervasia M. Schreckenberg and Harvey H. Bird, "Neural Plasticity Of MUS musculus In Response To Disharmonic Sound," *Bulletin, New Jersey Academy of Science*, Vol. 32, No. 2, Fall 1987, p. 81.
4. Ibid., p. 82.
5. Willi Apel and Ralph T. Daniel, *The Harvard Brief Dictionary of Music*, (New York: Simon and Schuster, 1974) pp. 68, 69.
6. Schreckenberg and Bird, op. cit., p. 77.
7. Edward Podolsky, *Music For Your Health*, (New York: Bernard Ackerman, Inc., 1945) pp. 26, 27.
8. Erwin H. Schneider, ed., *Music Therapy* (Lawence, 1959), p. 3.
9. Ira A. Altshuler, "A Psychiatrist's Experiences With Music as a Therapeutic Agent," *Music and Medicine*, (New York: Henry Shuman, Inc., 1948), pp. 270, 271.
10. G. Harrer and H. Harrer, "Music, Emotions and Vegetativum," *Weiner Medizinische Wochenschrift*. NR 45/46, 1968.
11. Willem Van de Wall, *Music in Hospitals*, (New York: Russell Sage Foundation, 1946); Ibid., p. 15; Harrer and Harrer, op. cit., pp 45, 46; Mary Griffiths, *Introduction to Human Physiology*, (New York: MacMillan Publishing Co., Inc., 1974), pp. 474, 475; Edward Podolsky, op. cit., p. 131; Doris Soilbelman, *Therapeutic and Industrial Use of Music*, (New York: Columbia University Press, 1948), p. 4; Arthur Guyton, *Functions of the Human Body*, 3rd ed. (Philadelphia: W. B. Saunders, 1969), pp. 332-340.
12. Michael Segell, "Rhythmatism," *American Health*, December 1988, p. 60.
13. H. Lloyd Leno, "The Power of Music," *Our Firm Foundation*, January 1987, p. 19.
14. Leonid Malnikov, "USSR: Music and Medicine," *Music Journal*, XXCII, November 1970, p. 15.
15. Coris Soilbelman, op. cit., p. 47.
16. Van de Wall, op. cit.
17. *American Mercury*, September 1961, p. 46; Ibid., p. 46.
18. Robert E. Ornstein, Ph.D., and David S. Sobel, M.D., "Healthy Pleasures," *American Health*, May 1989, p. 58.

19. Harold Shryock, M.S., Hubert O. Swartout, M.D., Dr. P.H., *You and Your Health*, (Pacific Press Pub. Assos., 1970), Vol. 3, p. 132.
20. Seminars given by: College Point Corporate Part., 129-09 26th Ave., Flushing, New York, 11356.
21. Murray Rockowitz, Ph.D., Samuel C. Brownstein, and Max Peters, *How to Prepare for the GED*, (New York: Barron's Educational Series, Inc., 1988) p. 9.
22. Carles W. Hughes, "Rhythm and Health," *Music and Medicine*, ed. by Dorothy Shullian and Max Schoen (New York: Henry Schuman Inc., 1948), 186, 187.
23. Michael Segell, op. cit., p. 59.
24. Max Shoen, *Psychology of Music*, (New York: Ronald, 1940), p. 89.
25. G. Harrer and H. Harrer, op. cit., pp. 45, 46.
26. Gervasia M. Schreckenberg and Harvey H. Bird., op. cit., p. 78.
27. Ibid., pp. 77-86.
28. Ibid., p. 84.
29. John 10:10

Chart 2

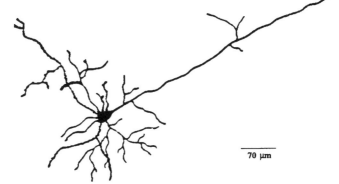

Figure 1. Camera lucida sketch of a representative
neuron of the C-group.

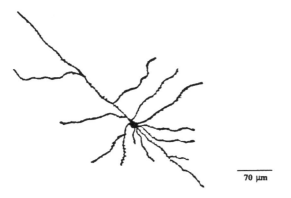

Figure 2. Camera lucida sketch of a
representative neuron of the H-group.

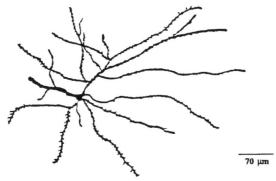

Figure 3. Camera lucida sketch of a representative
neuron of the D-group.

Chart 3

AUTONOMIC NERVOUS SYSTEM*

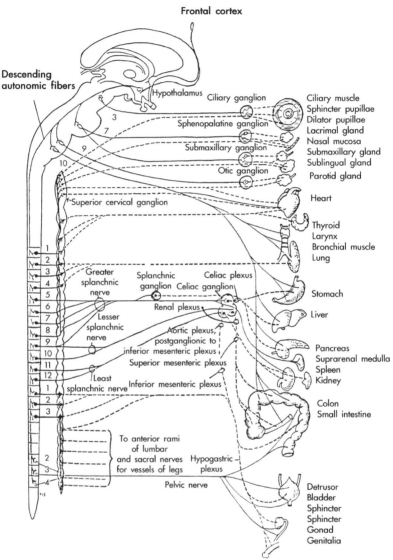

*Textbook of Anatomy and Physiology
(Catherine Parker Anthony, The C.V. Mosby Co.; p. 233).

Chapter 3

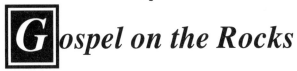

Gospel on the Rocks

During our first section, "Rock and Its Role," we spoke of the tremendous changes that took place during the '60s. But there were changes — vast changes — on another frontier of which we spoke not.

While secular America was rocking and reeling, religious America was also experiencing dramatic changes. Something very new and mysterious was happening. A "strange fire" swept over South America, then jumped the gulf to the United States, sweeping the country in what seemed like one mighty stroke. The new "flame" was charismatic Catholicism. Catholics all across the nation were experiencing the "spirit" manifestations of "tongues" with many Protestant groups following suit. The rapture theory, first conceived by a Jesuit Priest, Ribera of Salamanca, Spain, in the year 1585, became the new great Protestant awakening. Sensitivity sessions of touching, and "listening" were common as well as folk, rock, jazz, and gay mass. In a very short time, many Protestant churches did the same. (Remember, it has been the practice of the Catholic Church for many years to hold dances in the basements of their churches and schools. Many Protestant churches did also, so to bring in these new forms of worship did not appear that out of place or different from their usual practices, though a few years earlier, most would have vehemently denied that they would have ever "desecrated" their sanctuaries with such secular pursuits.)

Then, as it always does, it knocked on the front doors of our church. "May we come in?" The replies were many and varied. Some were shocked, others responded with less than Christian behavior. Many just watched, some with interest and others with indifference. Others prayed and sought the Lord. For a time, the voice that won out sounded something like this. "Please, let's not get too excited and do anything rash. Don't you think we need to show a spirit of love and tolerance, peradventure we might win a few."

Was it really something to get excited about, you know, the speaking in tongues, the very sudden influx of the "unkempt" look, the quick rise of rebellion with its inherent disrespect for authority, the music. Should we have responded with more resolution to know and follow God's will?

Some, who were keenly aware of the origins and evolution of this type of "spirit" movement (and I am including the music in this) were very concerned. Let us share with you why.

History of "Spirit" Manifestations and Its Corresponding Music

The Bible says that rebellion is as the sin of witchcraft, and so it is. Ever since Lucifer rebelled, his system of worship — devil worship — has been replete with witchcraft, and music as accompaniment and enhancement to the different temple rites which included wild orgies and "systems for the disturbance of consciousness."[1]

Modern historians, seeking to find the roots of such present day worship and music, trace its origins to ancient Egypt. From ancient Egypt, it then "spread to West Africa, including Dahomey [the seat of the Voodoo religion[2]] and the Congo."[3] Through the unfortunate slave trade, these forms of worship then spread from West Africa to the West Indies, (especially Hispaniola), South America, Inter America, and North America.[4] "Many African, Caribbean, and Native American tribes used *drums* as *sacred tools*, indispensable to

32

the rituals and ceremonies of tribal life. Their primitive percussionists learned to induce physiological responses, from *ecstasy* and *hallucinations* to seizures and unconsciousness."[5]

Nowhere in the United States was the influence of these pagan forms of worship felt more than in the territory of New Orleans. The music and dances of these rituals became a source of entertainment for tourists to New Orleans and many other cities as the numbers of those espousing these traditions moved across the land.

But for many "Christian" Americans, the pagan music, with its big polyrhythm drum beats and dances, was far too crude and vulgar to be tolerated. A real crusade began to convert the newest members of our society's family to Christianity. The result of this conflict of cultures was the birth of the "spirituals" and "gospel" songs.

The "new" sound continued to be blown about by many winds. As it was influenced by European musical tradition it also influenced with its rhythmical emphasis and dance styles. The unique rhythms of these dances "plus many other ingredients and entertainment practices (including Voodoo) combined to form a music called Jazz."[6]

"The most salient features of jazz derive directly from the blues. Jazz is a vocally oriented music; its players replace the voice with their instruments, but try to recreate its singing style and blue notes by using scooping, sliding, whining, growling, and falsetto effects."[7] "Trumpeters and clarinetists forced their instruments to sing the blues. . . In order to get the 'dirty' tones they wanted, they used an endless variety of mutes — plungers, cups, drinking glasses and pop bottles."[8] "Little attention was paid to 'correct' intonation. . . Instead, the players glided freely from one tone to another (or through long series of tones in glissandos) and frequently fluctuated the pitches of sustained tones (by using) a wide vibrato."[9]

"The black poet and writer Leroi Jones observed that performers. . . were deliberately making 'the instrument sound as unmusical, or as non-western as possible and reacting against the softness and "legitimacy" that had crept into black instrumental music.' "[10]

New Orleans was the perfect "breeding ground" for such developments. A busy port-of-call, it "overflowed with bars, taverns, luxurious and low-class bordellos, gambling dens, saloons, barrelhouses and honky-tonks. Each such place, each dance hall, owed it to itself to have its own pianist or group... In clubs such as these (the fashionable brothels), pianists like Jean le Baptiste and Tony Jackson... soon began playing, because the customers wanted their kind of music... Thanks to the reputation which the Negro orchestras began to enjoy, the doors of the dance halls and saloons of the 'District' were opened to them... After the parades, the burials, the election gatherings, the picnics along Lake Pontchartrain, evening dancing parties in the suburbs, the prodigious Mardi Gras festivals (where almost anything would go so long as it was noisy) the new music moved in where it was most welcome. Alcohol, love and dancing have always gotten along well together. The foot-stamping, the shouts, the syncopations, the screams, and heat of jazz needed the humus of Storyville (a forty-block vice district) to germinate."[11]

Due to the closing of Storyville by the United States Navy in 1917 and depressed economic conditions, large numbers of musicians went up the Mississippi to Memphis, and other river towns, and especially to Chicago, to seek employment. Still, their entertainment was kept to the centers of ill-repute.

"During the depression of the 1930s the music industry collapsed, and the classic blues singers and jazz musicians of the '20s died or retired. The next form of blues to find a broad popular market is usually called 'rhythm and blues,' and during the 1940s and '50s it was the dominant form of black popular music.[12] Of course, the blues had "always existed as a secularized form of gospel music, drawing not only musical ideas and techniques from spirituals and gospel songs but sharing the same feelings."[13]

34

"In the middle 1950s rhythm and blues became widely popular not only with urban Negro audiences but also with white teenagers. Immediately white musicians adapted the musical vocabulary and methods of rhythm and blues to their interests... A new group of white musicians directly influenced by... rhythm and blues... became new pop stars: Elvis Presley, Jerry Lee Lewis, Gene Vincent, Buddy Holly, [Bill Haley and the Comets, the first internationally famous group], and many more. The music was no longer called rhythm and blues, it became know as rock and roll."[14]

"As its name implies, rock and roll was primarily a dance music — the emphasis shifting from blues to rhythm — and it was accepted as a focal point for teenage life, a common bond, an outlet for aggressions, a standard to rally around."[15] Its insistent "basic backbeat and shuffle rhythms of rhythm and blues... demanded a physical response... So the harsh, direct syncopation of rock and roll came as a physical manifestation of its content — a challenge to loosen up, to break the old molds of convention and propriety, to express real emotions. The musicians themselves moved and danced as they played, begging the listener to cast off his inhibitions."[16]

"In the 1960s, rock became the characteristic popular music around the world. More than a musical style, rock became a social and political medium, the core of a lifestyle for a generation of young men and women."[17] "The 'language' of (this) rock culture encompasses musical and literary allusions from all corners of world culture."[18] Interestingly, rock music not only encompasses all cultures, it scatters such "allusions" to the four corners of society.

You can see that "rock has been a powerful channel for the forces of black music and the black experience... It has also amplified and disseminated black dance styles and feelings to the young... It has been an inherently revolutionary force, focusing on the problems and discontents of. . . civilization. It has brought a measure of self-liberation to the

young. . . It has also brought new miseries and problems —
despair, drugs, disaffections with all elements of stability and
tradition in life."[19]

As It Was — So It Is

Here we stand now, on the threshold between yesterday
and tomorrow. Looking back, we have seen that the "big beat"
was part of the package of ancient pagan worship. In fact it was
the "sacred tool" that made many of their experiences possible.
We followed it for thousands of years until it hit the shores of
"Christian" America. Here, for some time, it seemed that the
face of ancient paganism was going to experience a permanent
change, but the clamor for cultural identity with the forefathers
won out, and while once detested, then tolerated, then excused,
and now embraced, the "sacred tool" once again reigns.

"Yesterday" it prepared its participants for the temple
orgies. Today "its strength (has) always been rooted in the
sexual energy of its rhythms; in that sense, the outraged parents
who had seen rock as a threat to their children's virtue were
right. Rock 'n' roll made you want to move and shake and get
physically excited."[20]

"Yesterday" the music accompanied and encouraged
dances such as the "danse du ventre" in which "the shoulders,
buttocks, stomach and breasts are all separately or
simultaneously rotated, wagged or otherwise set in motion."[21];
and the Voodoo dances which featured "contortions of the
upper part of the body, especially the neck and shoulders."[22]
Today, you could easily use the very same description.

"Yesterday" it "altered consciousness" from mere "ecstasy
to unconsciousness." Today, the very same "highs" are being
experienced. Even "auditory driving" to the point of seizures
and unconsciousness is not uncommon.[23]

"Yesterday" it was part of the worship service, sacred
oblations to the gods. What about today? In the late '60s and early
'70s, this music found its way into the worship services of both

Protestant and Catholic churches. It was used to create a spiritual "high," an altered emotional state. There is only one difference — a big difference. Where it had been used only in pagan worship, now it is being used in "Christian" religious rites.

---

1. Pennethorne Hughes, *Witchcraft*, (London: Longmans, Green and Co., 1965) p. 23; Quoted by Ishmael Reed in *Mumbo Jumbo*, (New York: Doubleday, 1972), p. 191.
2. Marshall Stearns,*The Story of Jazz*, (New York: Oxford University Press, 1956), p. 20; Robert Tallant, *Voodoo in New Orleans*, (New York: MacMillan, 1964), p. 13.
3. Earnest A. Budge, *Osiris*, (New Hyde Park, New York: University Books, 1961), p. 245.
4. Eileen Southern, *The Music of Black Americans: A History*, (New York: W.W. Norton & Co., 1971), p. 3; Marshall Stearns, op. cit., pp. 19 and 37.
5. Michael Segell, "Rhythmitism" *American Health*, December 1988, pp. 58-62.
6. Robert Tallant, op. cit., p. 20; Marshall Stearns, op. cit., pp. 50, 51.
7. Eileen Southern, op. cit., p. 376, 377.
8. Ibid., p. 358.
9. Ibid., p. 376,377.
10. *The Sun-Herald*, March 19, 1989 (Australia) p. 148.
11. Andre Francis, *Jazz*, (New York: Grove Press, Inc., 1960), p. 30.
12. William J. Schafer, *Rock Music*, (Augsburg Publishing House, 1972), p. 15.
13. Ibid., p. 13.
14. Ibid., p. 15, 16.
15. Ibid., p. 16.
16. Ibid., p. 17.
17. Ibid., p. 13.
18. Ibid., p. 51.
19. Ibid., p. 12.
20. Janet Podell, *The Reference Shelf — Rock Music in America*, (The H.W. Wilson Company, New York: 1987), pp. 46, 47.
21. Earnest A. Budge, op. cit., p. 245.
22. Marshall Stearns and Jean Stearns, *The Jazz Dance*, (New York: Longmans, Grand Co., 1965, p. 19.
23. Michael Segell, op. cit., p. 61.

Chapter 4

*T*he Big Question

The Big Question

The entrance of religious rock into the Adventist church was slower than into many other churches because as a people, we were not accustomed to hearing these sounds due to our teaching against dancing, theater, and drama. Also, at that time television viewing was not so generally practiced as it is now. So its entrance had to be made with a music typical of the pre-rock era — the late '50s and very early '60s — which it did very successfully because we felt we needed to witness to and speak the same language as the new generation if we were to win them to Jesus Christ.

The question is: Can one clean up rock music, with its built-in means of tearing down standards, morals and judgement by placing religious words with it? Or is this a blending of the sacred with the profane, the holy with the common? (Ezekiel 22:25-28) If this is the case, is this not what the Bible speaks of when it refers to Babylon? Is it possible that we are accepting Babylon right into the only church that teaches "Babylon has fallen — come out of her my people"?

A second question needs to be asked: Has the church experienced, to a greater or lesser degree, the same changes of behavior and attitudes as is characteristic among other religious and secular groups? Is the rise of divorce and remarriage, the lower standards of piety and morality among many of the young, the spirit of insubordination to all levels of authority within and without the church, as well as to the authority of God and His prophets, the splintering of church doctrine in the multiple heresies we now have to attend to — are these evidences that we have experienced a marked downward trend? By 1868 the clarion of warning was loudly sounding. Music was playing a role in religious desensitizing of the youth. "They have a keen ear for music, [wrote the author] and Satan knows what organs to excite to animate, engross, and charm the mind so that Christ is not desired. Music, when not abused, is a great blessing; but when put to a wrong use, it is a terrible curse. It excites, but does not impart that strength and courage which the Christian can find only at the throne of grace."[1]

The Poisonous Mixture

You know, whenever this music has been coupled with the worship of God, whether within or without our church, it has always been accompanied by false doctrines. Take for example the strong early Pentecostal movements with their peculiar music and spiritualistic beliefs and demonstrations. Interestingly, this movement found its way into one of our campmeetings in Indiana. The year was 1900. Listen to some accounts of those meetings.

"They have a big drum, two tambourines, a big bass fiddle, two small fiddles, a flute and two cornets, and an organ and a few voices. They have 'Garden of Spices' as a songbook [a Pentecostal Hymnal] and play dance tunes to sacred words. They have never used our own hymn books except when Elders Breed or Haskell speak, then they open and close with a hymn from our book, but all the other songs are from the other book. They shout 'Amens' and 'Praise the Lord,' 'Glory to God,' just like a Salvation Army service. It is distressing to one's soul. The doctrines preached correspond to the rest. The poor sheep are truly confused."[2]

"Last Sabbath they took the early meeting, also the 11 o'clock hour, and called them front to the altar, as they call the little fence they have around the pulpit. The poor sheep came flocking up until they were on the ground three rows deep. The ministers kept up their shouting and, shall I call it yelling. They invited Elder Haskell and Elder Breed to come down to the altar and help. They went down, and Elder Breed got down and tried to talk to some, but he felt so out of place he got up on his feet and stood and looked on. Elder H. left the tent and went to our own tent. Finally they had a season of prayer, then they got up and began shouting, 'Praise the Lord,' 'Glory,' etc., falling on one another's neck and kissing and shaking hands, keeping their music going with the noise, until many of them looked almost crazy."[3]

It Will Happen Again

During the development of this strange movement, Ellen White was in Australia. She returned to America the same month as the last campmeeting which was September 13-23. When she arrived home, she found letters waiting for her concerning the experiences mentioned before. She wrote a response dated October 10, 1900. Portions of this response are very interesting in light of what we have been presenting here. We quote:

"The things you have described as taking place in Indiana, the Lord has shown me would take place just before the close of probation. Every uncouth thing will be demonstrated. There will be shouting, with drums, music, and dancing. The senses of rational beings will become so confused that they cannot be trusted to make right decisions. And this is called the moving of the Holy Spirit.

"... A bedlam of noise shocks the senses and perverts that which if conducted aright might be a blessing. The powers of satanic agencies blend with the din and noise to have a carnival, and this is termed the Holy Spirit's working.

"When the camp meeting is ended, the good which ought to have been done and which might have been done by the presentation of sacred truth is not accomplished. Those participating in the supposed revival receive impressions which lead them adrift. They cannot tell what they formerly knew regarding Bible principles.

"No encouragement should be given to this kind of worship. . . Satan works amid the din and confusion of such music, which, properly conducted, would be a praise and glory to God. He makes its effect like the poison sting of the serpent.

"Those things which have been in the past will be in the future. Satan will make music a snare by the way in which it is conducted. God calls upon His people, who have the light before them in the Word and in the Testimonies, to read and consider, and take heed. Clear and definite instruction has been given in order that all may understand. But the itching desire to originate something new results in strange doctrines, and largely destroys the influence of those who would be a power for good if they held firm the beginning of their confidence in the truth the Lord had given them."[4] In another reference to this experience she wrote: "These were carried away by a spiritualistic delusion. . . Should we carry out the plans that some would be pleased to have us carry out, companies would be formed who would bring in spiritualistic manifestations that would confuse the faith of many."[5]

Notice the scenario. Music was used to confuse the minds of otherwise rational persons. In this state they could not be trusted to make right decisions. They "received impressions which lead them adrift" and "they cannot tell what they formerly knew regarding Bible principles."

The most distressing part of this message is that it indicates that we will not have learned our lesson. We will repeat the errors of our past — especially in regard to music. "There will be shouting, with drums, music, and dancing, just before the close of probation." It is interesting that Israel of old had this very same problem just before entering the Promised Land. They were beguiled with music and then seduced to immorality and pagan worship. (See Exodus 32.) The Bible tells us that all this was written for our admonition. Are these prophetic admonitions seeing their fulfillment in our church today?

Are we hearing "dance tunes" with sacred words? Is there shouting? Are we hearing the drum beat? We may not be seeing it because Satan works very carefully. He knows the prophecies so he is hiding the drums in very small packages, namely commercially orchestrated accompaniment tapes, cassettes, records and CD's.

Are we close to the end of probation? You be the judge. All we ask is that for your sake, the sake of your church, and for God's sake — to whom we are most precious — please consider these things carefully and prayerfully, and determine to be found among those who will hear the words: "Welcome Home, Children, ye who have been faithful in little things and I will make you ruler over much. Enter into the joy of thy Lord!" (Matthew 25:21)

---

1. Ellen G. White, *Testimonies for the Church*, Vol. 1, p. 497.
2. Hetty H. Haskel, Letter to Miss Sara McInterfer dated at Muncie, Indiana, September 17, 1900.
3. Haskel, Letter to Ellen G. White, dated at Muncie, Indiana, September 22, 1900.
4. Ellen G. White, *Selected Messages*, Vol. 2, pp. 36-38.
5. Ellen G. White, *Evangelism*, p. 595.

Chapter V

R *ocking the Boat*

Without question, the issues raised in these pages are sensitive and to many, very personal. Church musicians, pastors, youth pastors, and teachers, struggle over the question of appropriate music. Accusations and counter-accusations fly, wounding hearts and lives and most sadly, the heart and body of Christ, His church. Is it really necessary to rock the boat?

Be assured, this book was not written to be used by anyone or any group to be destructive or cruel. We must, however, realize that truth, if it is truth, can rarely be applied to any human heart without doing some cutting away. We are still sinners in need of a Savior, and as long as there is life, the growth and sanctification process should still continue.

Every time we present this subject, we ourselves are reminded that we need to ever become more consistent in the application of these principles to our own music presentations and concurrently, more understanding of the struggles of others.

The following few lines deal briefly with the questions and observations that most often are raised when we present our seminar on music. Perhaps you will find some of these items helpful as you consider what your personal response should be to the information herein presented.

1. We agree with you, but what can we do?

First, realize you are only responsible for that which you are given authority over. That always includes yourself. Choice is always yours; no one can take it away from you.

True, your choice may bring scary results, even death, but you can always choose.

After you take care of yourself, if you are a family head, your responsibility will include **your** family. If you are a Sabbath School department leader, **your** department... and so on. If you are a church board member, you are under Christian obligation to speak what you are convicted the truth to be. (Remember, the attitude is just as important as the message.) You are under obligation to vote your convictions. But if you are voted down, you are not responsible for the outcome. If, however, you did not speak your convictions or vote them and the board makes a wrong decision, you do share the blame. This is true at every level of administration.

One may need to write a note of request to the governing committee at the level of initial complaint. But once the note is written and sent, nothing more should be said or done unless you yourself have a position of trust on the committee addressed. (If the nature of the problem is very serious, one might need to appeal to a higher committee, and even up to the highest. If the results are not what you think they should be, remember, God does not hold you responsible for what you do not have authority over.)

What about having to listen to objectionable music in church? If the issue is properly addressed as outlined above and no changes are made, you have two options:

a. If the music is not too loud, simply read the Bible or otherwise place your mind on heavenly things and consciously refuse the music entrance. This **can** be done.

b. If, however, it becomes too much of a struggle or the music is too loud, you may need to look for a more appropriate place to worship. If that becomes necessary, do so quietly and without rancor. And please remember, even if boards vote incorrectly, it is still individual members who are wrong, not the "church." As a church, we have excellent policies on music printed in *Guidelines Toward a Seventh-day Adventist*

Philosophy of Music, Department of Education, General Conference of Seventh-day Adventists. The guidelines are there. It is the people — who either don't know, or don't care, or don't feel it is important enough, or are afraid, or genuinely or not so genuinely feel that times have changed and so should the guidelines — who don't implement the principles we already have.

2. **What about music committees — why do they seem to be confused and problematic?**

The good news is that not all music committees are problematic. The sad reality is that many are and usually the reason is that the members approach the subject of music from the point of personal likes or dislikes or personal feelings. This only pivots one against another. If our committees could agree on guidelines based on principles, and apply those guidelines consistently, it would not be easy, but it would be clear and fair. One caution: Remember that if you think you can decide whether a piece of music is acceptable or not by the way it affects you, you are on a dead end street because once you begin to listen to the music critically, your mind overrides the autonomic system, thus suppressing the physiological responses until after you quit listening to the music critically. The practice of listening critically is what gives rise to the all too familiar response, "It doesn't affect **me** that way!" (Based on chapter, "Rhythm Rules," footnote 25.)

3. **What about that observation, "It doesn't affect me that way"?**

Studies clearly show that people of all races and all cultures respond physiologically and mentally in nearly identical ways. **What does change is a body's defense.**

Let me illustrate. A young person smokes for the first time. Unless his environment is grossly polluted, his body will react to the poison by coughing and dizziness. As he keeps smoking, his defense becomes paralyzed by the constant bombardment leading him to state triumphantly that smoking doesn't bother him anymore. The truth is that he is in the ultimate state of deception. All warning signs are gone and will remain so, most often, until it is too late to save his health, if not his life.

Likewise with music. We thought the Beatles were the "screaming kids from Liverpool" when they first appeared on the scene in the early '60s. Have you listened to those songs lately? They sound like ballads. Why? Our body's defense has become numbed and it takes stronger and stronger "poison" to rally the defense mechanisms. But the workings of your body — the lack of a harmonic environment — is taking its toll. It is breaking down your nerve balance and affecting your whole autonomic system. These are the facts.

And remember, those of you who smugly say you would never listen to "that hard stuff" — no one but the rawest of pagans ever started with the hard stuff first. We all start with the easy. Though the use in lesser degrees seems to have its benefits, it really is no reason for boasting. It is where you are headed that matters; not how fast you are getting there or how far you **haven't** gone.

4. It's our culture!

This is one of the most common defenses and presently a very sensitive issue.

Even though music is such an integral part of every culture, the truth is, the question of culture and music has no relationship. The physiological effects of music are the same whether you are red, yellow, black, or white, regardless of your origins and upbringing.

One has to think of music like wine. New wine — pure grape juice — if taken in temperate amounts is very good for any and everyone. Alcoholic wine destroys brain cells, impedes reaction time, distorts judgment regardless of how much or how little you drink or who you are. One shot of alcohol destroys ten to fifteen thousand brain cells. Obviously then, the degree of damage is directly proportionate to the amount of alcohol imbibed and one's own physical weaknesses, but all are physiologically affected adversely.

Other considerations: In the Bible, the closest discussions to the present meaning and use of the word culture are verses that deal with customs and traditions. Such verses as Matthew 15:3 and 9, Colossians 2:8, Leviticus 18:30, and Jeremiah 10:3 make it clear that in God's eyes, any custom or tradition which does not have as its origin the mind of God and the principles of heaven simply is not acceptable behavior for a child of the heavenly King.

How many of us, in defending our culture, are showing a preference for our earthly roots over our Divine (see Luke 3:38 — Adam, the son of God). And how many of us are showing that we would rather identify with our past citizenry than our future as potential citizens of Heaven.

Keep in mind, anything good in any culture is the result of the influence of God's ways. Conversely, all customs and traditions even slightly divergent from truth, Godly culture, or the laws of nature, are of the evil one. There are only two fathers, only two paths, only two destinies. There is no middle ground. Limbo is not biblical!

Without question, the **counsel** of the Bible is cultural, not reflecting the cultures of man, but the true culture (refinement) of God. However, many of the **lives** described in the Bible reflect human culture mingled with Divine. David is a very graphic example of this with his many wives and other obviously non-Godlike characteristics. That is why our example is not even the great men of the Scriptures but rather Jesus, the God-man. How sad and confusing the outcome when we search the Scriptures for what men did or didn't do rather than for the counsel of God. The stories are given for us to understand God's way of dealing with sinners: the counsel, for a light unto our path. Let's be careful we don't confuse the two and thus be clinging to the earthly weaknesses, even of the children of God, in place of the heavenly pattern.

5. David danced! And what about the 150th Psalm?

a. Many of the injunctions of the Psalms were intended to be implemented in and during the festivals — in the streets, not in the sanctuary (e.i. clapping, dancing, cymbals, etc.). We forget that the whole culture of the Jews, handed to them by God, was to remind them of God, to keep in their hearts a thankful, joyful attitude toward the goodness of God and His laws. **All social activities were religious in nature.** They were celebrations, like the Feast of Tabernacles. What was acceptable in these festivals was not necessarily acceptable in church (consider the difference between the festivals and the Day of Atonement). There is a big difference in Scripture between celebration and worship. One was outside the house of God, one inside. One under God's watchful eye, the other face-to-face. One, joyful and playful, the other awesome and reverent. Remember also, when Isarel was worshiping the golden calf, it sounded to Moses like the sounds of a festival ("noise [voice] of them that sing [answer, respond]" Exodus 32:18).

b. The word "dance" has more than one meaning in Scripture. It most often means "chorus" and is also used a lot for the actions of skipping and leaping for joy (David's experience). It is not always clear what meaning is intended by the verses themselves or even the Hebrew or Greek. But it is clear that the word has meanings that are far more innocent and pure than what we often try to read into them; "solemn gladness" as E.G. White refers to David's rejoicing in *Patriarchs and Prophets*, p. 705. The Jews put much scripture and experiences to song and chorus, many of which were choreographed and performed at the numerous festivals and victory celebrations.

c. The problem is not the instrument, but how and where

the instrument is used. A drum can be used to keep time as Miriam did with the "tambourine" (a hand drum used in Bible times) for that great multitude of ladies in their festivities, or, it can be misused, even in social gatherings, to give overemphasis to rhythm and unnatural beats — thus the need of drum sets. Ellen White's reference to drums is obviously addressing the latter misuse. (See Chapter IV, pp. 40-41.)

Obviously, the questions herein addressed do not encompass all the inquiries concerning the subject of music. But our goal is to awaken in the reader a deep desire and responsibility to weigh carefully the question of music and its influence.

The Lord has promised, "…thine ears shall hear a word behind thee, saying, This is the way, walk ye in it, when ye turn to the right hand, and when ye turn to the left." Isaiah 30:21.

Appendix

Elements of Music

(Refer to Chart 1 on page 17.) **Sound in music** usually has a definite **pitch** that we describe as "high" or "low". A musical sound, called a **tone**, is produced when something causes a series of vibrations that recur a certain number of times each second. For example, heavy wires that vibrate slowly, only 32.7 times a second, produce the lowest C on the piano. The thin wires that produce the highest C on the piano vibrate more then 4,000 times a second, or almost 130 times as fast as the lowest.

Musical tones also have other characteristics. For example, some tones are long and some are short. We call this the duration. The same tone, played on different instruments, has different tone colors. This is the **quality** of the tone. Some tones are loud and others are soft. We call this the **intensity** of the tone. A tone often has other tones that support and accompany it. These other tones form its **harmony**. If a series of tones make up a tune, we may call it a melody.

A **scale** is a series of tones arranged according to rising or falling pitch. The piano keyboard has a regular pattern of white and black keys. The distance from one key to the next, whether black or white, is always a half step. The half step above any white key is called a sharp, and the half step below any key is called a flat. Composers use many kinds of scales. Most scales are based on the octave, except in Oriental music. An **octave** (named for the Latin word for eight) is the interval between two tones of the same name. The higher tone has twice as many vibrations per second as the lower, so the relationship is based as much on physics as on art.

As in illustration we use the piano, an instrument which is tuned to **equal temperament**. This means that the intervals between tones have been made uniform. Each black key stands for two notes, such as C-sharp or D-flat. Actually, these notes are not precisely the same. Equal temperament permits a keyboard instrument to be of practical size and still play in reasonably accurate tune in all keys. A stringed instrument without a fretted fingerboard, such as the violin, permits the player to produce C-sharp and D-flat as separate tones.

Melody is a succession of musical tones - in its simplest form, a tune. We remember a beautiful tone more for its melody then for its words. A melody consists of a series of tones played in a fixed pattern of pitches and rhythms. It may be repeated, expanded, or varied, according to the composer's wishes.

Harmony is other tones heard with a tone which strengthen it, often helping set its mood. Composers create harmony in music with **chords,** which are groups of three or more related tones sounded at the same time. Chords are built on the scale and the physical properties of the tones themselves.

The chords and harmonies in a piece of music are usually based on the same scale. We can say that they are in the same tonality (sometimes called **key**). The name of the scale on which the work is based is drawn from the tone on which scale starts (such as C or F), and also from whether the chords are major or minor.

For the last 500 years, composers have usually used a harmonic system based on the tonic and dominant tones of the scale. After fixing the tonic tone and home key firmly in the listener's mind, the composer may **modulate** (shift) into the key in which the dominant of the "home" key becomes the new tonic. Modulation adds variety and may emphasize a contrasting section of his work. After the composer finishes the contrasting section, he usually returns to the "home" key.

Rhythm may be considered as everything that has to do with the duration of the musical sounds. Accent is an important factor in musical rhythm. The composer usually builds his music on a pattern of regularly recurring strong and weak accents. This pattern of accents permits the music to be divided in to units of time called **measures** or **bars**. Weak accents help build the rhythm by creating anticipation for the strong ones. **Tempo** is the rate of speed at which music is played. It is related to, but not a part of, rhythm. A change in tempo can often change the meaning of music. **Tone color** is one of the most elusive qualities in music. Human voices may sing the same range of notes, yet produce widely different sounds. Different choices of chords give varying colors. Various instruments affect the tone color of the music they play. A melody may seem dark and mournful when played on the English horn. The same melody may sound bright and happy when played on the flute or violin. Tempo and rhythm are also factors in the effect a melody has on us.[1]

---

1. Taken from the *World Book Encyclopedia,* 1976, article on "Music," Vol. 13, pp. 788-790.